M

Church on the Water
Church of the Light

D1560701

Phaidon Press Ltd
Regent's Wharf
All Saints Street
London N1 9PA

First published 1996

© 1996 Phaidon Press Limited

ISBN 0 7148 3268 5

A CIP catalogue record for
this book is available from the
British Library.

Printed in Singapore

Church on the Water
Church of the Light
Tadao Ando

Philip Drew
ARCHITECTURE IN DETAIL

1

From the heartland of Japan

Tadao Ando is very physical person. He is continually animated. When talking to you his hands move constantly; suddenly he will pick up a coloured pencil and start to sketch. He is restless and compact – like a boxer in the ring he keeps moving. Ando's eyes smile back at you; they dance around you as though sparring and then reach out and clasp you momentarily as if to weigh you up, taking you in a grip that feels almost physical it is so intensely focused. Tadao Ando has a certain closeness, he experiences things and people in a tactile way.

Some people keep their distance when they meet new people. Not so Ando – he advances toward you. He is both centred and lively and his architecture can be thought of in the same way: his buildings instantly engage you, there is no way to avoid a response, they are so strongly formed, such insistent tectonic constructions. The walls, floors and ceilings, with their carefully placed openings and slots, are simultaneously metaphysical as well as physical instruments of his architecture.

It comes as no surprise to learn that Tadao Ando began his adult life as a boxer.

He is still boxing, only now he throws up walls the way some fighters throw punches. His walls hit you with the force and precision of a well-placed blow, and draw a clear boundary around his buildings. They are more than a barrier between inside and outside, for this isolation of the interior from the exterior marks a beginning not an ending. Ando's bounded domain is a very human space which assists people to develop and to be themselves.

From boxing, Ando learned that surprise gives a fighter an important advantage. This is something he shares with Alvar Aalto, who, when young, learned from a street-fighter friend the value of catching an opponent off guard. Indeed, one of Aalto's mottoes was, 'take them by surprise' – that is, always do the unexpected. Aalto turned the element of surprise into a lifelong architectural strategy. For Ando, the boxer turned architect, surprise is more than just a habit, it is a plan for dealing with design problems.

Osaka, Ando's home, is Japan's second largest city after Tokyo, and much older. Osaka borders the Inland Sea in the Setouchi-Kinki or Kinki region. This was the first area to be developed and is the heart-

1 The calm of Tadao Ando's architecture is belied by his physical presence – he is an intensely energetic and mentally focused individual and this shows immediately.
2 Osaka, Japan's second largest city, is a sprawling giant without an obvious centre.
3 Tokyo, by comparison, is chaos with a still centre as its focus.

2

3

4

5

4 Tokyo never stops: at night, a
blaze of neon signs, traffic, create a bizarre world of bars, clubs
and restaurants, as work gives
way to pleasure.
5 The Osaka skyline is generally
flatter than in Tokyo, its tight grid
of streets produces a dense
horizontal matrix of buildings, a
uniform chaos interrupted
by expressways.
6 The seventeenth-century
Yoshimura House: its elegant
arrangement of white rectangular panels within dark timber
frames, integrity of material, and
subtle adjustment of daylight is
close to Ando's architecture.
7 Light filtering through the high
window of the nineteenth-cen-
tury Habakino House makes us
aware of the emptiness within.

land of Japan. Kyoto and Nara are close by: Kyoto is 45km to the north–northeast with Nara just 30km to the east. Whereas Tokyo was the city of the warrior and the Shogun, the Meiji and Emperor, and is now the centre of government, Osaka continues to be a city of merchants. It began as a fortified city and developed, mainly because of its central position with regard to sea traffic, into the commercial and industrial hub of Japan. Whereas Tokyo assumed a circular shape around Nihonbashi and the castle with the streets extending radially from the centre, Osaka, by contrast, followed the ancient Chinese system of rectangular blocks. The merchants' houses were concentrated near the harbour indicating the importance of sea trade. It is now a city of endless rows of factories and frenetic activity. The 1989 film *Black Rain* showed it at its raw and ugly worst.

Working in Osaka, Ando enjoys greater freedom than he might in Tokyo. Architecture in Tokyo is often arbitrary and just a little crazy. It frequently seems outrageous, being calculated to attract the eye in a city where buildings compete for attention and where anything odd or bizarre has a distinct advantage. This jumping to extremes is all to do with the competition to be first, with everyone racing to catch the next wave; yet it is a race in which no one is quite sure what that next wave is likely to be about – and like so much else in Japanese life the winning post is continually shifting. Architects read constantly and watch one another. None of the architects knows for certain the general direction in which they should be travelling, so they run around in circles looking for it. Tadao Ando in Osaka is removed from this competition, and this freedom is precisely what makes him special. Moreover, Ando is a very self-reliant person.

Even as a child, Ando came into contact with the great classics of minka and traditional Japanese architecture. The magnificent seventeenth-century Yoshimura House at Habakino in Osaka Prefecture is not far away from the architect's practice. Without even being aware of it, Ando was exposed to this older tradition. This is apparent in his symbolic reliance on the wall and his preference for architectural compositions based on simple arrangements of squares.

6

7

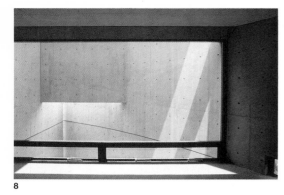

8

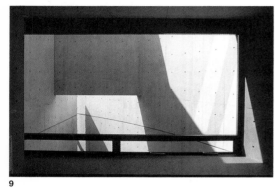

9

8, 9 Ando's Oyodo atelier: the interiors of Ando's buildings are continually changing, depending on the day, the season, with the shifting play of light patterns.
10 This futuristic twin tower by architect Hiroshi Hara, in a style recalling Sant' Elia, was intended to give Osaka an appropriately dynamic symbolic focus.
11 Ito House, Tokyo, 1990. The protecting wall penetrates the main volume of the building in the form of a half-circle arc, defining the entry space of the house.

10

11

As an architect, Ando is self-taught; he never studied at a university school of architecture. For a short time he was apprenticed to a carpenter, but in 1962, he set out on travels that took him to the USA, Europe and Africa, which lasted until 1969. It was during these formative years of travel that he took to looking for the same qualities in the architecture of the West he had earlier encountered in Japanese farmhouses and townhouses. What had impressed him most was the effect of light filtering through the high windows into farmhouses in the snowy north of Japan. The sharp contrast of light and shade in the streets of medieval Italian cities reignited this memory. It revealed to Ando a richly realized world of unadorned forms and architectural spaces in which there was a real intimacy with the lives of ordinary people.

Ando's rise to prominence has been rapid. Many factors have been at work but one in particular helped considerably. Kenneth Frampton, a comparatively new Professor at Columbia University and the architectural adviser for the publisher Rizzoli in New York, became aware of

Ando's architecture in the early 1980s, at about the same time that he was advancing his arguments on 'critical regionalism'. From this point of view, few other architects were better placed to illustrate his thesis, and Ando's architecture thus provided an exemplary demonstration of Frampton's ideas.

What most concerned Frampton was the worldwide spread of a mediocre homogeneous architecture by means of a phenomenon of universalization that signified not only a subtle destruction of traditional culture, but also represented an attack on the creative nucleus of the great cultures that form the basis of our interpretation of life itself.[1] Frampton was searching for something that would mediate the impact of a universal civilization with elements indirectly derived from the peculiarities of each region. He thought this would be made possible by, '… such things as the range and quality of the local light, or in a tectonic derived from a peculiar structural mode, or in the topography of a given site.'[2] Frampton stressed the importance of establishing a clearly bounded domain. He considered he might best resist the

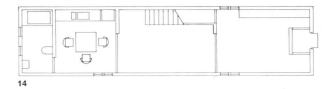

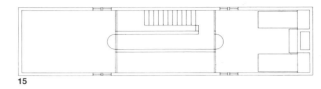

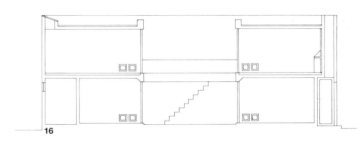

12 Matsutani House, Kyoto, 1978. This house by Ando was an attempt to create pure architectural space; compositionally, it consists simply of two blocks separated by a courtyard.
13 Azuma House, Sumiyoshi, Osaka, 1975–6. On the outside, Ando has repeated the facade unit of the existing row houses, while inside, the space is divided into two cubic blocks with a courtyard in between, connected by a bridge.
14–17 Azuma House plans, section and axonometric.

14

15

16

7

12

13

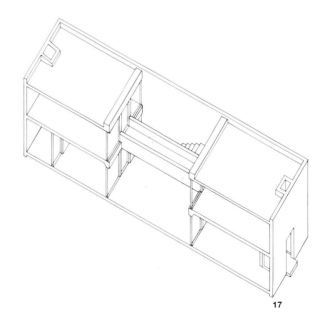

17

universalizing effects of technology by emphasizing the particular qualities of place-form and by invoking the capacity of the human body to read the environment in ways other than the visual.

In his book *Modern Architecture: A Critical History*,[3] Frampton lamented the fact that modern architecture suffered from a 'distancing' from its environment: 'This self-imposed limitation relates to that which Heidegger has called a "loss of nearness".'

Frampton's arguments almost perfectly meshed with what Ando was then doing. Ando's early work, after he opened his office in 1969, consisted principally of small houses built in the Kansai District and quickly came to reflect the regional vernacular of the area. This regional strain in the work was quite unconscious but nonetheless apparent, and nowhere was this more so than in his 1975–6 Row, or Azuma, House at Sumiyoshi, which was subsequently awarded the 1979 annual prize of the Architectural Institute of Japan.

Through his prolific writings, Frampton gained wide international recognition for Ando's achievements; and although It would be unfair to Ando to infer this was the sole factor at work, it undoubtedly helped. In 1985 Ando received the Alvar Aalto Medal; then, in 1989, the French Academy of Architects honoured him with its Gold Medal; and this was followed in 1992 by the Carlsberg Architectural Prize from Denmark.

The secular and the sacred
The Church on the Water and Church of the Light were designed in the years between 1985 and 1988. Building work did not start until mid-1988: the Church on the Water was completed very quickly in five months; the construction of Church of the Light taking eleven months. The Chapel on Mount Rokko, near Kobe, Hyogo, in 1985–6, preceded them. These are mature works, coming after the international recognition signalled by the Alvar Aalto Medal. The two churches explore the dimension of sacred space, and appear different, yet their differences are more apparent than real. Before 1980, the majority of Tadao Ando's work had consisted of small houses. These were mainly of a closed spatial type, although there were some that were open, and a few that mixed the two spatial orientations. The

houses of the late 1970s gradually acquired – almost reluctantly it might be suggested – an outward orientation that left open the possibility of eventually establishing a connection with the surrounding urban environment, without in the least bit compromising their essential centripetal character.[4] Indeed, Ando invested the secular private domain with aspects of the sacred.

Ando's work springs from the subconscious and finds an affinity with Zen philosophies while it is also connected with a deeper current in Japanese tradition. Through his work, Tadao Ando expresses the dual nature of existence. At the intersection of light and silence we become aware of 'nothingness', a void at the heart of things. Ando's houses, including his secular works, have this sacred quality which is more pronounced still in his church buildings.

One of the leading features of Ando's interiors is their profound emptiness. This can be disturbing at first, challenging as well as puzzling. The spaces have an unmistakable quality of poverty and stillness which is another way of describing tranquility. It is tempting to think of this as inspired by Ando's interest in modern architecture since a kind of spatial emptiness also arises in the two dimensional abstract pictorial spaces of Elementarism. In Tadao Ando's architecture 'emptiness' means something different, however – it introduces us to the spiritual dimension, to the 'Godhead'.

In Zen, and Zen art, 'being' is considered to be the self-unfolding of the unformed 'Nothing' or 'God'. In particular, the function of the beautiful is to spark an epiphany of the absolute and formless void which is God. True emptiness is the state of zero. This is expressed by the equation zero equals infinity, and vice-versa. Accordingly, emptiness is not literally a lack of content or passivity. It is 'being', and it is 'becoming'. It is knowledge and innocence. In architecture this means that perfect poverty is attained when perfect emptiness attains perfect fullness. Or, to put it another way: when 'nothing' becomes 'everything'.

As a piece of logic this is contradictory. It is only when we ourselves experience the richness of emptiness directly in spaces such as the Church on the Water and the Church of the Light that the psychological reality implicit in the assertion is fully registered.

18

18 Ando's Rokko Housing, 1981, is built against a steep hillside to the north of and overlooking Kobe.
19 Each apartment looks out across a south-facing terrace towards Kobe and the Inland Sea.
20 The housing is embedded in the mountainside with a street running up the centre from the bottom to the top.
21 Walkways at each level link the apartments to the central street.

20

21

19

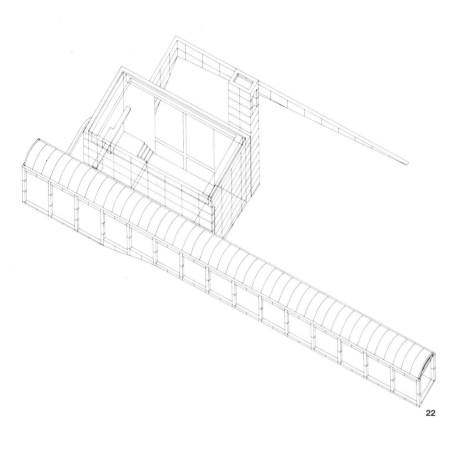

22

22, 23 Chapel on Mount Rokko, Kobe, 1985. Located on the verdant slope of Mount Rokko, the chapel itself consists of two cubes reached by means of a long covered gallery.
24 Chapel on Mount Rokko, elevations and sections.

9

23

Because the Godhead is defined in Zen as a flowing together of all things in the 'nothing', in this equation, 'suchness' coincides with 'emptiness'. However, 'nothing' in this context is the precise opposite of the nihilism with which it is often confused in the West. On the contrary, Ando treats emptiness as a kind of divine fullness which is absolutely life-affirming. He is concerned with an inwardly echoing aesthetic poverty, a quality of simplicity which is encapsulated in the Japanese term *wabi*.

Ando's architecture reveals that the kind of emptiness he creates is intended to focus our vision by the elimination of anything extraneous which might divert our attention from what he sees as most real – that is, the essential quality of the space. Paring away his architecture in this way, reducing it to the simplest of terms, using a simple geometry of cubes and cylinders, bare concrete walls, solids and voids, light and darkness, Ando hopes to confront us with emptiness, with the Godhead. This is as true of his secular buildings as it is of the two churches. Light is the special medium which he uses to clarify the emptiness in his architecture.

The cosmic cube

The two churches represent a climax in which certain themes, present to some degree in most of Ando's work, are highlighted; in his terms, dwelling is not something separate but is inextricably linked to the sacred. Both church and house require the creation of a fixed point – a centre from which we orientate ourselves in the world, from which we go forth, and to which we return. Setting aside space, wresting the sacred from the mundane, requires that certain conditions are fulfilled. This notion finds a parallel in the opposition between inhabited territory and the unknown and indeterminate realm around it. The house resembles our own world, a cosmos, outside of which is chaos. This notion is fundamental to Ando's architecture. The Japanese city is a disorderly territory; it represents chaos, in contrast to the house which signifies a centred cosmic world. This begins to suggest the reason why Ando places so much stress on walls, why his spaces are so strongly centripetal in orientation, and why the quality and direction of light is so important.

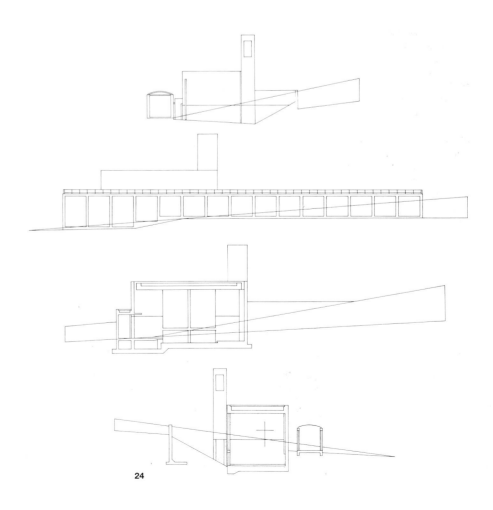

24

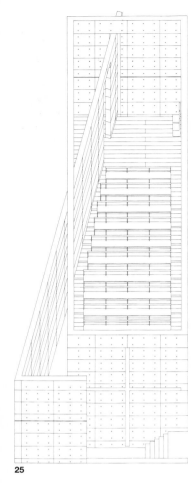

25

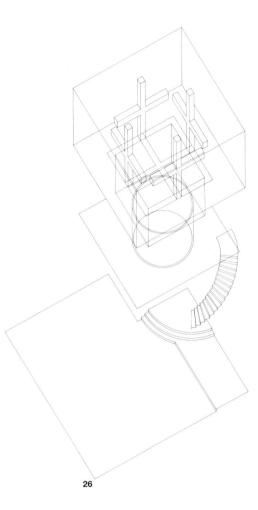

26

Space in Ando's buildings is strictly organized by means of simple geometric relationships. The Chapel on Mount Rokko, for example, is a neat square in section made up of two 6.5m cubes (6.5m wide x 13m long x 6.5m high); the Church of the Light consists of three 5.9m cubes (5.9m wide x 17.7m long x 5.9m high); while the Church on the Water is more complex, here the large 15m square space of the chapel is overlaid by a smaller 10m square on one corner which it overlaps by 5m. The pool in front consists of two 45m squares (45m wide x 90m long). The proportion of each space can be reduced to a simple ratio: 1:2:1 in the case of the Chapel on Mount Rokko, 1:3:1 for the Church of the Light, and 3 x 3 + 2 x 2 for the Church on the Water.

In drawings, the simple geometric composition of each scheme is indicated by circles.[5] These represent spheres. According to the ancient Greek philosopher Timaeus, the elements of the material world were not earth, air, fire and water, but two types of right-angled triangles. Above them were four or five solids from which all matter was constructed. The earth, we are told, was constructed of cube-shaped atoms. In order

to make his architecture cosmic, Ando first chose the sphere, but since this had obvious practical difficulties he simplified it to a cube.

Where the internal space is highly geometrically organized, with integers determining the proportions of the spaces, this is at a symbolic level, paradigmatic of the cosmos. It is accompanied by a similar heightened perception of *ma* or 'nothingness'. The purpose of this is to make the individual aware of an absolute reality that transcends his being in the world. Thus, Ando's houses found the world by their geometry, by being centred, and by the use of light. The thick concrete walls keep out the chaos of the city. Why are Ando's houses designed in this way? Why must they resemble sacred space? In essence, what Ando is saying through the medium of his architecture is that humans cannot live in chaos; architecture therefore has a responsibility to create an ordered world. Ando's churches are therefore an excellent way of introducing his architecture. To create a centre is to build a world. In doing so we establish the necessary pre-conditions for dwelling.

Because the universe unfolds from the centre and stretches out towards the four

25 Church of the Light, axonometric. The volume of the building which is equivalent to three cubes, is penetrated on the long side by an L-shaped wall which exits at the back.
26 Church on the Water, axonometric. The lower, larger 15m square of the church is overlaid by a smaller 10m square on one corner, and the two are connected by a stair.
27 Ando's Naoshima Contemporary Art Museum, 1992. Chaos is interrupted by embedding geometric forms in the land.

27

28

29

28, 29 Kidosaki House, Tokyo, 1986. The abstractness of traditional Japanese domestic architecture provides an inspiration for the present.
30, 31 The Koshino House, Ashiya, 1981, was particularly successful in its use of light, with its dramatic play of light patterns revealing the tactile quality of the concrete surfaces.

11

cardinal points, Ando placed four crosses on top of his Church on the Water on each side of a 10 metre square. These define a centre constructed as a paradigmatic model of the world of the gods. In the Church of the Light, the cross-shaped opening at one end becomes the door to the world above, through which the gods can descend to earth and man can symbolically ascend to heaven. Allied to light, which symbolizes the divine, the austere expression of the cross as an opening in the wall makes it a kind of communion with heaven, an opening through which a symbolic passage is possible.

Homage to the wall

The importance given by Ando to walls is a distinct departure from modern architectural practice which typically downplayed the wall in the 1920s. In his 'five points' statement of 1926,[6] Le Corbusier distinguished between the structural system which carried the intermediate ceilings and rose up to the roof, and the interior walls which no longer supported the other elements of the building, and were henceforth regarded as membranes to be placed with total freedom wherever they were needed. When taken with the free design of the facade, which also lost its load-bearing role, walls could become thin elements or transparent planes. With the advent of Elementarism, walls were treated as separate vertical planes around which space flowed in a fluid and dynamic way. Mies van der Rohe's Barcelona Pavilion of 1929 was perhaps the most famous exemplar of this type of Elementarist space.

Ando's revival of the wall as a fixed containing element as well as his rejection of open universal space is contrary to Modernist architectural prejudices and also raises questions about the human significance and symbolic meaning of the wall. Indeed, his preoccupation with solid walls is close to an obsession. Ando's walls are usually made of in-situ poured concrete. They are static and permanent, and whilst considerable care is taken to see that they are as perfect as technique allows, they are massive. The main reinforced concrete shell of the Church of the Light is 380mm (15in) thick, while the external wall of the Church on the Water consists of two skins – a 250mm (10in) outer skin of concrete, 50mm

30

31

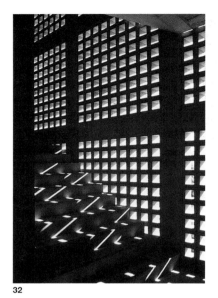

32

(2in) thickness of insulation to guard against the intense cold, and a 600mm (24in) thick inner skin, making it in total 900mm (36in) thick. A smooth surface was achieved by adopting a dense engineering quality mix with a slump less than 15cm (6in) and by ensuring thorough vibration with a minimum cover for the reinforcing bars of 5cm (2in) to avoid weathering problems and staining. The density of the concrete results in a glass-like surface that registers the different qualities of light, and this tends to dematerialize it. Because Ando's concrete is so precisely wrought, so smooth and reflective, it produces an illusion of a taut, textile surface rather than presenting itself as a heavy earthbound mass.

Ando has his own teams of expert carpenters to make the formwork who compete against each other; even so, his walls contain imperfections and are uneven. Nevertheless, his resuscitation of the wall and the return to a more traditional interpretation has important consequences.

Light is invited to play across the surface of the concrete, constantly revealing as it moves the ever-changing interdependency of light, climate and season across time.

To this end, Ando inserts vertical slots in his walls. He does the same with the roof slab, separating it from the wall with channels so that light can pour in at an incident angle in a way that reveals every minor alteration in plane, and models each curved surface in delicate chiaroscuro. Ando's walls state their thickness and density, but they also have another purpose which is to establish a human zone for the individual.

The oldest known wall found so far, in central Israel, is nearly 6,000 years old. Walls kept the weather out, but they were also a defence against other humans – they framed boundaries between territories and prevented movement. Until the eighteenth century, it was customary to build cities within a defensive wall. Indeed, a wall was a labour-saving device because it took fewer defenders to keep out an enemy.

In Homer's *Iliad*, the Achaians besieging Troy built a wall as a defence for their beached ships and for themselves.[7] The ancient Greeks employed walls as an aggressive military weapon. During the Athenian seige of Syracuse in 414BC, the Athenians ran a wall behind the Syracusan position to cut them off; no sooner had they

32 'Festival', Naha, 1984. The staccato of light from a glass block wall falling on a stair is at once abstract and modern, at the same time that it recalls the traditional shoji screen.
33 Church on the Water. The four crosses on each side of the square are joined together at their feet by a cross infilled by frosted glass blocks.
34 Church of the Light. The inwardness of the church is relieved by the splayed wall breaking through the side bringing outside light with it.

33

34

35

36

37

35 The contrast between Ando's geometric order and chaos is especially powerful in the peninsular siting of the Himeji Children's Museum, 1989.

36 Josef Albers, *Homage to the Square*, 1959. The artist's composition of squares within squares becomes a kind of monotonal mandala for Ando.

37 In their earliest Buddhist temple complexes (this temple dates from 607AD) the Japanese copied Chinese systems contained within a rectangular wall marking off the sacred from chaos.

38 Church of the Light interior with the cross end wall removed. This illustrates the degree to which conceptually architecture has been transformed into something extremely abstract and based on a rigorous all-pervading geometry.

done this than the Syracusans retaliated by building a counter-wall.[8] Victory was decided less by strength of arms than by the extent of each army's walls. Many walls, notably Hadrian's Wall between England and Scotland, and the Great Wall of China in the Han and Ming periods, were a permanent defence against invasion. In China the ideas of 'city wall' and 'city' are closely related, as use of the same word for each, *ch'eng*, indicates.[9] The very first act in building a city was to raise a wall around it.

There are a number of things in Ando's architecture, such as his use of walls vis-à-vis the outside world to confer individuality, together with the repetition of the circle and square in his plan forms which are suggestive of Chinese architecture. The importance attached to the wall by Ando, for one, revives traditional values which have their origin in China. There, the wall was the most essential and permanent feature of the Chinese city and its buildings, and the house, which turned a blind wall toward the street and opened to a courtyard, was the typical cell of society. The walls of Peking were an important frame that enclosed and limited the city. In fact, the whole city is a

series of large and small squares – in Chinese architecture space is conceived as a series of imbricated squares. Traditional Japanese architecture inherited the Chinese mode of closed spaces which was transplanted in the early Buddhist precincts grouped around Heijokyo in the Yamato District (Nara).

Chinese architectural space is a series of closed worlds, and is founded on geometry. In the Chinese universe the earth is considered square and heaven round. These two shapes provide the basic geometrical framework for Ando's buildings. His architecture is a synthesis of opposites, bringing together concepts from the East and the West. At the same time, Ando chose Josef Albers's manipulation of squares in his *Homage to the Square* series to formulate his own spaces. This arrangement of squares within squares constitutes a kind of monotonal mandala. It results, as he has explained, in '… an architecture that has been transformed from something extremely abstract and constructed according to a rigorous geometry to something representational and bearing the imprint of the human body'.[10]

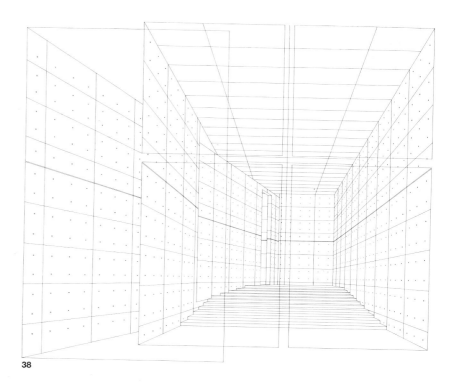

38

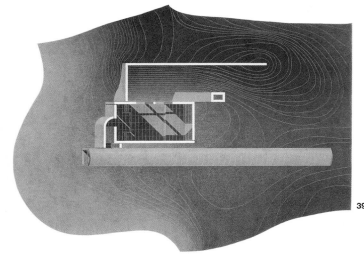

39

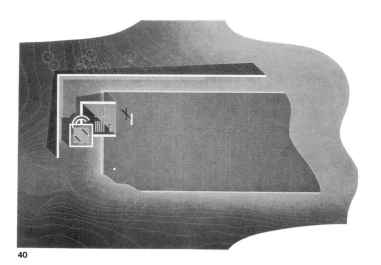

40

39–41 The Church of the Light, Church on the Water and Chapel on Mount Rokko all repeat much the same formula of a chapel body surrounded by an outer L-shaped wall that marks out the extent of sacred space.

Inside the labyrinth

The Church on the Water is surrounded by two sets of walls. These walls establish a frame around a closed entity, but this frame is deliberately incomplete. A large L-shaped concrete wall on two sides separates the church and the pond terraces from the surrounding landscape and clearly establishes a boundary for the church precinct. The pond, which is divided into four terraces in 150mm (6in) steps, introduces yet another horizontal frame which slides underneath the building. This third frame which overlays the church is designed to connect the building with its surroundings. On the west and south it was initially contemplated that there would be a break in the strict rectangular geometry formed by a natural water edge which would remind man of the presence of nature. The idea was to have nature give a subtle nudge to the strict formal geometry of the composition. The church is a square, walled off and enclosed within a larger rectangular frame. The glazed side facing the pond can be opened completely by sliding the entire wall to one side. Ando has written: 'In the West,

a sacred space is transcendental. However, I believe that a sacred space must be related in some way to nature, which has nothing to do with animism or pantheism.'[11] By framing nature with walls, Ando seeks to geometricize it to make it more abstract. Its abstraction corresponds to man's will, and it is this which makes it sacred. The name of the church recognizes this. The church space floats above water and is further linked to it by an external cross which stands in the first water terrace.

The separation of sacred space from the chaos around it occurs to much the same extent in the Church of the Light. In this instance, however, the deployment of the walls is more involved and complex. Here, an angled wall cuts through the long west side of the main chapel at 15 degrees and exits through the end wall. This wall hooks back on itself next to the street and obscures a section of the altar elevation. Balancing this, a third low L-shaped retaining wall encloses the entry court. Walls on this occasion provide frames that isolate the sacred space from its immediate surroundings, indicating that it is a world in

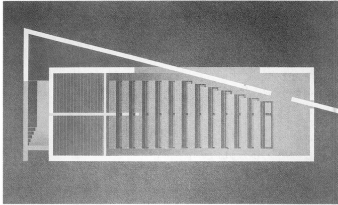

41

42

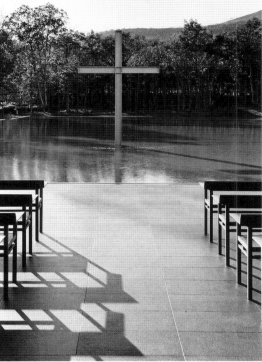

43

itself. The churches are detached representations of that cosmicized world rather than part of it.

In Japan, most forms of spiritual exercise take place in close proximity to nature. Normally, Ando's architecture focuses in on itself which can give it the appearance of turning its back on nature. His aim is to create spaces that are alive, that are single shells on the outside and labyrinthine inside, into which nature is drawn. Walls are agents of this internal world. The forms used in the architecture are simplified to the point where we are tempted to forget them altogether. The internal spaces behave as complex sundials aided by such contrivances as skylights, slits and curved walls, which, when seen from the inside, give the impression of being buried in the earth. In this respect, light, not the solid concrete walls, is the principal goal of the architecture.

In both churches Ando took on the challenge of bringing nature *inside*. He wanted man and nature to confront each other within the enclosed, internal world of his architecture. This involved creating a tension between the two which is expressly resolved in the 'nothingness' of the internal space. To achieve this Ando conceived his buildings almost as land art, buried places that struggle to emerge from the earth, which, by their struggle, dramatize the encounter between architecture and nature.

The cross is the leading symbol in both works. The Church of the Light is a functioning Christian church on the outskirts of Osaka that serves the local Ibaraki community. The Church on the Water is a Western-style wedding chapel for honeymooning couples at the northern Tomamu resort on Hokkaido.

In order to draw nature inside, Ando found it necessary to lead his architecture to nature; the large pond in front of the Church on the Water links the two. The external cross outside the building in the water extends the symbol beyond the architectural frame. The cross cut out in the concrete wall at the front of the Church of the Light is a variation of this same idea. Looking at the cross one sees beyond it in one's imagination, while, because the interior is so contained the space tends to implode. It is as if the pressure inside falls and air swirls in through the open cross from the outside.

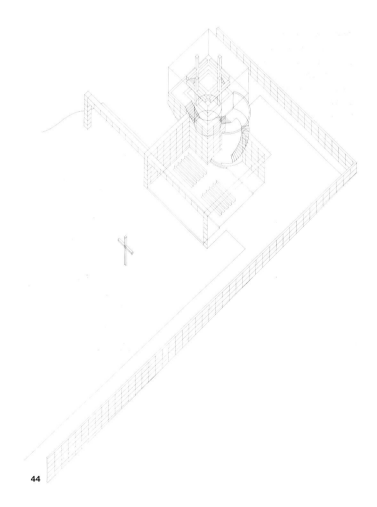

44

45

The four crosses mounted inside the glazed cube above the Church on the Water offer a three-dimensional version of this phenomenon. The transparent wall around the crosses is a reminder to us of the form from which the four crosses were carved. This powerful gesture sets one's minds to work mentally reconstructing the original cube. Standing inside at the centre and looking out between the crosses, the viewer is surrounded by four figures which frame the landscape of the surrounding hills and woods.

This use of the cross as a symbolic form in the landscape has a long history in Europe and there are corresponding gestures in traditional Japanese architecture. The *torii* in the bay at the Itsukishima shrine on the island of Miyajima beside the Inland Sea is a most impressive example of the projection of a frame in nature which simultaneously pulls the bay into the shrine.

In Europe, crucifixes were frequently erected in Catholic countries as a memorial or an object of pilgrimage in the landscape. In his paintings *The Cross in the Mountains*, 1807–08, and *Morning in the Riesengebirge*,

1810–11, Caspar David Friedrich depicted this type of crucifix. In the former image, the cross is on a hill-top with the figure of Christ on the crucifix facing the dying light of the setting sun. *The Cross in the Mountains* expresses a sentiment of transcendental pantheism, while in *Morning in the Riesengebirge*, the crucifix appears in the clear light of sunrise in a serene windless landscape from which all turbulence and disturbance has been removed. Here, the purity of the light and infinity of the horizon bring God closer.

The architectural elaboration of this motif makes its appearance in the Woodland Crematorium at Sockenvagen outside Stockholm, 1940, by Gunnar Asplund, and later in the Chapel of the Technical University at Otaniemi, 1957, by Kaija and Heikki Siren. This latter example is the direct precursor of Ando's Church on the Water. In Gunnar Asplund's Forest Crematorium, a monumental cross was erected on rising ground some distance beyond the portico of the main chapel. Mourners glimpsed it on their way to the crematorium. Asplund introduced an influential innovation in a bronze and glass

45 The appearance of the cross in the landscape has a long history in Europe which has parallels in Japanese architecture.
46 The *torii* in the bay at Miyajima marks the gateway in the seaward procession towards the temple shrine, but seen from the temple building, extends it out into the bay.
47 Caspar David Friedrich gave Christ's crucifixion a specifically northern context and relevance, here shown in a detail of the painting *Morning in the Riesengebirge*, 1810–11.
48 Friedrich's *The Cross in the Mountains*, 1907–08, expresses a transcendental pantheism merging into nature.

47

48

46

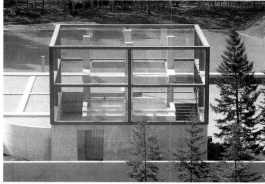

50

49

49 With the glass wall slid to one side, the chapel becomes a veranda-like space concentrating our attention on the primary focus – the crucifix in the pond.
50 All five faces of the upper cube have crosses; only the top is left open to accept the vertical sacred axis.
51 The Technical University Chapel by Kaija and Heiki Siren, Otaniemi, 1957: relocating the cross outside and placing it in a forest clearing changes our whole perception of this space.
52 At Gunnar Asplund's Woodland Crematorium, Stockholm, 1940, the cross is employed as a sign in the landscape, introducing the crematorium chapel seen beyond in the distance – the very opposite of the Siren's building.

17

door of the church which can be lowered into the ground to unify the space of the building and the court. Hence, the Church on the Water incorporates ideas from both buildings in its use of the external cross framed by the forest trees and the removable wall.

However, it was the Siren's Otaniemi Chapel that had the greatest influence on Ando. The placement of the cross outside the church beyond the altar is the one thing that contributed most to increasing the identification of the building with its environment. It leads, as in the Caspar David Friedrich paintings, to a pantheistic religious expression in which nature is made the primary focus of the chapel which assumes a dependent status as a shelter joined to, and serving, the cross in its beautiful setting. The stained timber screen-wall around the entry forecourt was repeated in the Church of the Light. Here, an L-shaped concrete wall leads worshippers around the church to the entrance.

In following the Siren's precedent, Ando did not necessarily accept its pantheistic premise of god in nature so much as reinforce the traditional Japanese idea that all forms of spiritual exercise benefit from

contact with nature. This affinity between Finnish and Japanese attitudes towards nature is also revealed in some of the early works of Alvar Aalto.

Ando's buildings force people to confront nature. This produces a kind of electrical charge between architecture and nature; depending on how you choose to read it, it either leads us out into the landscape, or draws nature inside. Either way, nature and architecture form a duality which Ando holds in tension as a simple opposition. In both the Church of the Light and Church on the Water, this duality is brought to the fore as a focus of religious feeling by freeing the chief symbol, the cross, and removing it to the outside so that it is included in nature, but still functions as the essential and central sign of the architecture. Removing the cross from the interior of each church, far from diminishing its power, actually increases its impact.

Light and darkness
The Church of the Light is a rather small building, hidden by pine trees, on the corner of two streets at Ibaraki. It is located 25km north–northeast of Osaka in the western

51

52

foothills of the Yodo valley railway corridor linking Osaka with Kyoto. The residential streets around it are quite narrow. The church itself is comparatively small having an area of 113sq m (1216 sq ft) – about the same size as a small house.

The building took more than two years to complete. It is used for classical concerts and community meetings as well as holding Christian services. The delay in completing the work was due to problems in raising the necessary funds. Initially it was feared that it would cost more than the budget and Ando even considered building it without a roof, but the construction firm donated the roof and this move became unnecessary.

Access to the church is intentionally indirect. Worshippers are required to enter the site at the northeast corner off a side street via a forecourt which leads around a corner of the church to the minister's house. From here, the route about turns and skips forward in a convoluted 'S' movement that takes the visitor through an opening in the long wall of the church and leads on to a second 1.60m wide by 5.35m high doorway in the angled blade wall. This is disorienting and creates a feeling of apprehension and

heightened expectation about what will follow next. One is soon rewarded by the wholly unexpected impact of the cross of light filling the surrounding darkness at the opposite end of the church.

The difficult entry serves to emphasize the movement across the threshold from the outside into the sacred interior. It has a similar effect to the 'kneeling in' entrance of the tea house which was intended to inculcate humility in all who enter. Ando's attitude to materials is also similar. In the tea house materials are plain and undecorated, colour and texture resulting directly from the nature of the materials used. As in the tea house, there are few openings inside the church, and these, with the exception of the cross opening at the front, admit a soft, diffused light. The floors and seats are made from rough timber planks of reclaimed scaffolding boards – this lowered the cost substantially. The choice of a natural material such as timber for the seating also relieves the coldness of the concrete and lends an overall feeling of warmth to the interior. Ando prefers to use natural materials where they come in contact with people because they are so tactile.

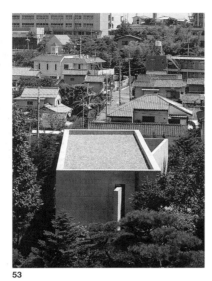

53

53 The Church of the Light is relatively small, hemmed in by housing. Its simple shoe-box like form is punctured by a single wall angled at 15 degrees which re-emerges at the back.
54 In a surprising reversal of Christian customs, the floor of the church steps down towards the altar; this lifts the congregation up in relation to the dominance of the cross-opening in the wall.
55 A screen of pine trees on two sides shields the building and acts as a foil to the brutal simplicity of its cubic form.

54

55

57

58

19

56 The church's arrangement repeats the basic composition of the concrete tea house of the Yamaguchi House, 1982, with its cubic body penetrated by a free-standing L-shaped wall.
57 Abbey at Sénanque, Provence. On the outside, this twelfth-century Cistercian abbey consists of two intersecting walls which are concentrated where their axes intersect.
58 The effect of the plain tunnel-vaulted interior of the Abbey at Sénanque depends almost entirely on the effect of light.
59 Ando's sketches clearly demonstrate his aesthetic idea which was a telescoping volume expanding towards the cross and lifting so as to indicate the point where the vertical and horizontal lines intersect in the cross.

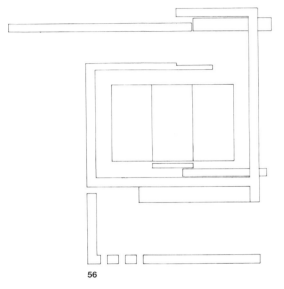
56

Once inside, the eye takes time to adjust to the gloom. Besides the cross punched out of the front wall, which in any case is only 20cm wide, a second full-height glazed opening is provided towards the rear where the diagonal blade of concrete slices through the side of the building. This helps to soften the contrast between the brilliant light of the cross and the darkened interior. The cross opening in the end wall is the principal daylight source, although this is supplemented by four small light fittings on the opposite wall. Light is reflected off the ceiling and walls by the glass-like concrete which helps to distribute the light more evenly.

Despite its traditional eastern end and radiant light, the form as a whole stems as much from the concrete tea house which Ando added in 1982 to his Yamaguchi House at Takarazuka, Hyogo, 1974–82, as it does from the more familiar model of the Western basilica. Ando has written that it was inspired by the Abbey at Sénanque in Provence which he visited in the 1960s.[12] The mixture of Eastern and Western motifs is fairly typical – Ando often deploys oriental and Japanese types with countervailing Western paradigms. It arises from his goal of fusing opposite spatial concepts into a fluid transcendental architecture. This is also about the integration of two opposites, abstraction and representation. (Moreover Ando himself is a twin which might help to explain his fascination with pairs of ideas.)

Early designs for the church showed the floor plan with pews in the middle and side access, which has not in fact been followed in practice. The church is split down the middle by a central aisle in line with the cross. The rows of seats are arranged on ten 10cm high by 90cm deep stained board terraces and the floor descends towards the altar. The cross opening symbolizes the intention of extreme economy imposed by the small budget.

The windows employ the same grey metal section used throughout Ando's work. For the cross, the 16mm float glass is fixed in the concrete without a frame to heighten further the dramatic effect of the light streaming through it. A horizontal groove, 3.95m above the floor, runs around the walls both inside and outside to coincide with the height of the underside of the

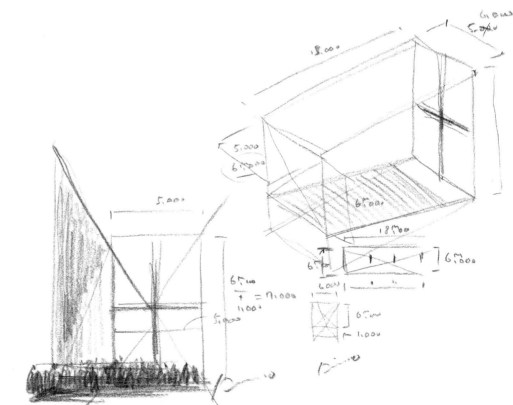
59

cross transom. An 18cm high gap has been left below the ceiling and the top of the angled blade wall. This separates it from the body of the church and expresses it as an autonomous and distinct element of the architecture.

Because it is so introspective and closed, the interior is strongly focused on the cross of light. The minister stands at a lectern on the right hand side from where he gives the lesson and directs the service. He preaches from below rather than from the more conventional elevated position above the congregation; it took Ando some time to persuade the minister and congregation on this point.

Water and sky

The Church on the Water is a much larger work. It is exactly three times the size of the Church of the Light with an area of 345sq m, and was designed well before it in mid-1985. Work did not commence until early 1988, but when it did it progressed very rapidly. The Church on the Water is located at Tomamu on a plain northeast of the Yubari Mountains which lie to the east of Sapporo on the northern island of Hokkaido.

The church is sited in a large clearing in a forest of beech trees on a sloping site that falls gently towards the nearby river. A low hill with a chair lift to the west dominates the prospect. A resort hotel complex is located behind the church to the east. Approximately 400 metres away northwest of the Church on the Water, an open amphitheatre is planned, although this building has not yet been realized. This facility has an anticipated capacity of about 6,000 seated in a semi-circular shaped bowl overlooking a fan-shaped artificial lake. It was intended for concerts in the warmer spring and summer seasons, while in winter the lake will become a skating rink. The Tomamu region is covered with snow from December to April when it is transformed into a beautiful white expanse.

Ando linked the two facilities, first, by a wall that points towards the church, and second, by the river lower down which bounds the large pond along its western edge. Water is diverted from this river into the 80m x 42.7m pond. The Church on the Water is set at the opposite east bank at one end of the pond on high ground.

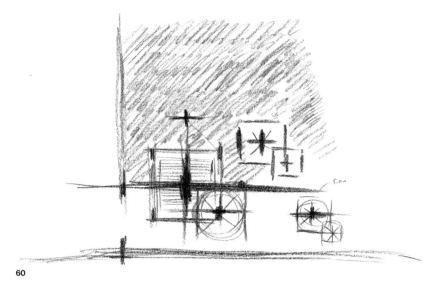

60

61

60 This sketch shows a somewhat different conception – the two overlapping squares are there, as is the pond, and including the outside wall, but the overlapping motif is repeated on the right leading into the pond.
61 The site of the chapel falls gently towards the nearby river seen in the foreground. Behind it lies the resort hotel complex.

62

The building consists of two squares, one 10 metres square and another 15 metres square; the two overlap in plan at one corner and are aligned along the same longitudinal axis as the pond. This asymmetrical group is framed by a 39.45m x 75.425m long freestanding L-shaped concrete wall on the east and south which serves to isolate the church from the hotel behind it.

The wall obscures the pond terraces which are glimpsed only after the visitor has rounded the wall at its extreme northernmost point. The rectangular water terrace is framed at this point by the 6.2m high flying beam-and-column wing used to support the glass wall which extends 15.9m out from the church. A modest entry is provided in the base of the glass cube through a doorway in the exposed concrete, and a deliberately circuitous approach takes the visitor down outside the L-shaped wall on the south and back up to the rear of the chapel. From here, the visitor is led up over and around four crosses which face one another across a square transparent glass roof made up of 16 panels of 15mm thick laminated float glass supported on

250mm deep H-section steel beams above the waiting-room level at the rear of the building. The circular-shaped lobby below it has a second glass ceiling in 6mm thick float glass.

The cube of light, with four crosses inside it, is connected to the main chapel by a dark semi-circular concrete stairway which protrudes from the back wall of the church in a cylindrical bulge. The 15mm float glass screen surrounding the crosses lifts the eye towards the sky framing it as it does so. Within this glass cube, the visitor is enveloped in light. The glare from the main window-wall was counterbalanced in the Siren's Chapel at Otaniemi by a large window behind and above the congregation. At Tomamu, the glass cube has replaced the rear window, but it no longer assists in reducing the glare of the window-wall at the front of the church. It becomes just another element in a dramatic sequence of controlled 'light experiences', as one passes from the brilliant light of the open sky on the exposed platform with its four crucifixes, to the darkened confined stairway leading down into the church, and thence, into the protected cave of

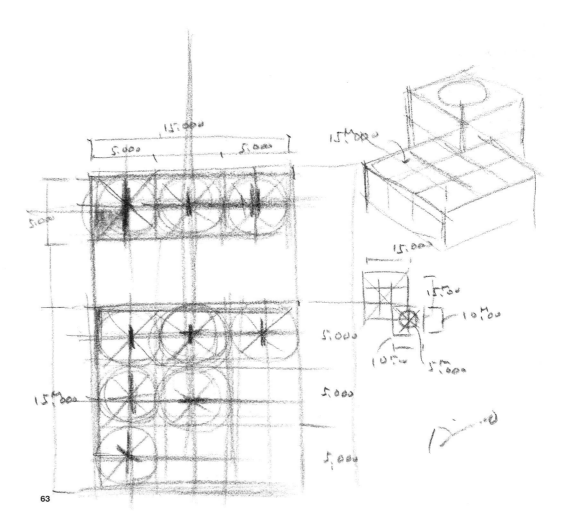

63

the chapel. Its open front looks directly out across the horizontal expanse of the water which in turn bounces light into the interior space where it is trapped.

As has already been noted, the glazed wall facing the pond slides open, exposing the interior to the outside and thereby producing an entirely new sense of intimacy with the church's surroundings. The heavy glass wall travels on an I-section steel track housed inside a massive inverted U-shaped steel structural beam. The marriage celebrants can feel they are outside while at the same time they are protected by a roof. The space, like a cave or gallery, parcels off a small fragment of universal space that is more in keeping with the human dimension. Opening up the church in this way creates an ambiguity which is much like that experienced inside a veranda, raising a sudden doubt as to the certainty of inside and the distinctness of outside.

The transparent cube of the four crosses draws the sacred vertical axis down to earth and spins it around so it darts from the building out into the landscape. The lower level, with its facilities for dressing, serves as a transitional lock. The four crosses are 50cm square in concrete and stand in a 6.5m square which is divided symmetrically into four 2.5m smaller glazed squares. The walkway, which consists of two up and two down stairs, circumambulates this quadrille of crucifixes. There is a stairway on each side, two up and two down, leading up from the entry then back down to the circular stair access to the chapel. The glass wall surrounding the crosses is supported by an H-section steel frame on the inside, and C-sections on the outside; all the steelwork is rustproofed and coated with fluorine resin. The glass screen is made of 15mm thick float glass. Directly under this is a translucent cylindrical-shaped glass antechamber with sliding doors giving access to three waiting rooms and male and female lavatories arranged around a cylindrical glass lobby.

The main chapel is relatively uncluttered. There are five rows of brown-stained timber bench seats in pairs on either side of the centre aisle. These are simply made up of horizontal and vertical members. The arm- and back-rests are subtly curved in a manner that invites the hand to touch them. The rear of the church on one side is taken

64

64 The framing effect of the building is increased at night by illuminating the cross and the adjoining beech forest.
65 Its abstract geometry utilizes the impact of single-point perspective where every line is made to converge on the centre of the cross.

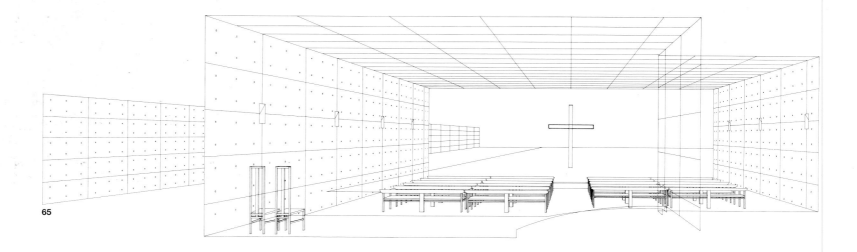

65

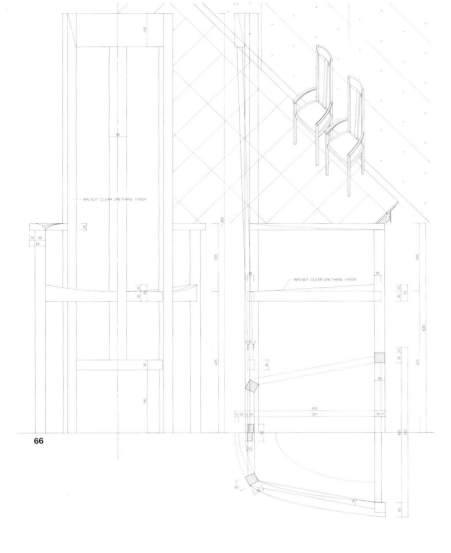

66

67

66, 67 Two chairs designed by
Ando have been placed at the
rear of the church.
68 In its two aspects, the building succeeds in bringing the vertical sacred axis at the back into
collision with the horizontal earth
axis entering from the front.

68

up by the dressing area which overlaps the chapel and from which issue three circular steps which press forward into the main space. With the exception of two Ando-designed chairs at the back, the opposite side is empty. The floor is covered in black granite slabs.

Bringing the divine to life

Ando has written: 'I want to give nature's power a presence in contemporary society and provide thereby the kind of stimulating places that speak directly to man's every sense as a living, corporeal being. More-over, retrieving from history's strata not form or style but the essential view of nature and life that runs through its depths – the spirit of culture, in other words.'[12]

What role do these churches serve? What is the function of the sacred in this? The sacred reveals to us what it means to be good and challenges us to be better human beings. It introduces the spiritual rising up out of life and gives it a heightened signi-ficance by its gesture of setting aside a special realm. In these two works by Tadao Ando ordinary materials are ennobled and given new meaning in ways that we least expect; he introduces the temporal dimension of sunlight and so makes us more aware of things through his disposition of walls and openings. Thus we are sensitized to nature, to shadows and the wind, to the sounds around us, to what it means to be fully alive to where we are.

By harnessing geometry, Ando centres people and creates the perfect circumstances for people to dwell in the world. The sacred is present in all his work to some extent; in these buildings only more so. The Church of the Light and Church on the Water complement each other. Two countervailing ideas are juxtaposed in the crucifix and the empty silence of the void as a sign of 'nothingness' – the sign of the West against the non-sign of the East. In the Church of the Light, the cross is a void drawing God inside its emptiness; in the Church on the Water, this is reversed – four solid crosses facing out in the four universal axes that orientate us. One is simple, but complex in its simplicity, the other is complex, yet simple in its complexity. They are constructed from within like a tea house. That is their special secret.

Church of the Light (right)
Entry to the building from the
narrow side street is indirect and
far from obvious.

Church on the Water (far right)
View from lowest water pond
with the freestanding beam
housing the track for the horizontal sliding wall visible to one
side of the church behind the
external cross.

Photographs

Church on the Water

View from the northeast corner
over the building to a low hill on
the west. Below the church is
a small river which defines the
southern boundary of the
water ponds.

Church on the Water
(left) Side elevation of the building behind the outer enclosing wall which returns across the hillside. The entrance to the church is partly visible below the upper cube frame containing the four crosses.
(right) Only when past the end of the wall is the entrance fully visible in the concrete base.

Church on the Water
(left) Detail of the top of the
concrete base and stair wall
with the cubic space frame
above it.
(right) Entrance to the church is
at the rear with stairs leading
onto the top of the smaller upper
cube of crosses.

Church on the Water
(left and above) Below the four
crosses is a cylindrical-shaped
antechamber with alcoves; waiting rooms and lavatories are
located around it. The photo-
graph above shows the underside of the translucent glass roof.
(right) Above the vestibule two
pairs of concrete crosses
confront each other within a
steel cubic frame.

Church on the Water

(far left) The displacement of the
steel cross in front of the open
interior in the first of the ponds
draws the space out into the
landscape.

(left) A semi-circular stair leads
down from the entrance to the
rear of the church.

(above and right) There are
five rows of pews of brown-
stained timber on either side
of the central aisle.

Church on the Water

(below) The beam carrying the
sliding track for the glass wall
also doubles as a frame for this
view of the ponds. The cross can
be seen on the far left.
(right) Side view across the
upper pond in front of the
church.

Church on the Water
(above) The church seen
shrouded in snow in the winter,
with the glass sliding wall behind
the cross closed.
(right) View from the south
below the church shows the
side extension of the facade to
accommodate the horizontal
sliding glass wall, with the
smaller upper cube containing
the freestanding concrete
crosses above it on the left.

(right) Rooftop view: the building
is hidden by foliage and the
roofs of nearby houses.
(far right) The end wall with its
cross-opening is framed by a
screen of trees between it and
the street.

Church of the Light

(left) Inside, behind the end wall, light flooding through the narrow cross aperture is reflected on the smooth concrete walls and ceiling.
(right) View across the church towards the front from the entrance on the right in the splay-wall.

Church of the Light
(left) View of the entrance in the splay-wall as it penetrates the rear of the church through an opening.
(right) Pews on the right side beside the opening; the splay-wall slides past into the church space.

Church of the Light

(far left) Detail of the window and splay-wall at the line where it breaks through the wall plane. A gap has been left below the ceiling and the top of the splay-wall.

(left, above and right) Light seeps through the narrow slots in the walls and is reflected by the smooth concrete which has a glass-like finish.

Church of the Light
The cross motif is repeated in
the ends of the timber pews and
is caught by beams of light as it
crosses the floor, evoking an
austere atmosphere, yet calm
at the same time.

Church on the Water

Site plan

(Ando's proposed Theatre on
the Water is shown to the north
of the church)

N

0		50m

0		150ft

Elevation

Section

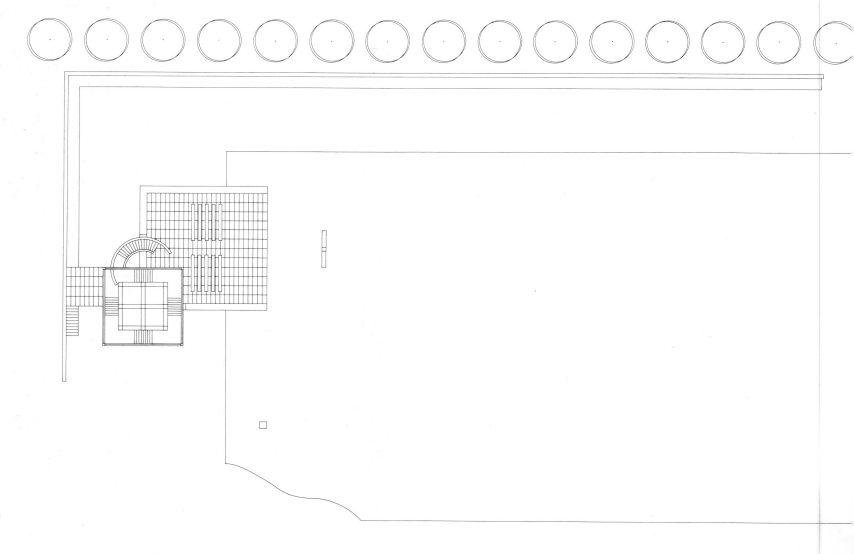

N

0   10m

0   30ft   **Plan**

**First floor plan and
details of movable screen**

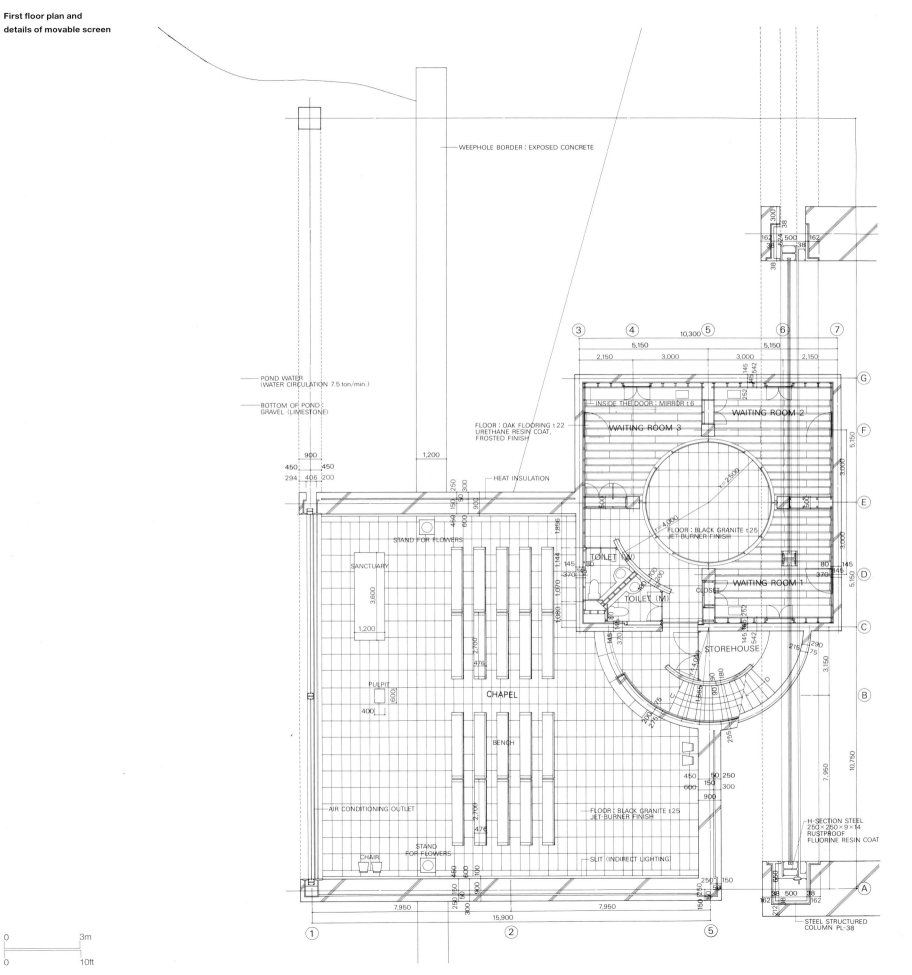

WEEPHOLE BORDER : EXPOSED CONCRETE

POND WATER
(WATER CIRCULATION 7.5 ton/min.)

BOTTOM OF POND :
GRAVEL (LIMESTONE)

FLOOR : OAK FLOORING t 22
URETHANE RESIN COAT,
FROSTED FINISH

HEAT INSULATION

INSIDE THE DOOR : MIRROR t 6

WAITING ROOM 3

WAITING ROOM 2

FLOOR : BLACK GRANITE t 25
JET-BURNER FINISH

STAND FOR FLOWERS

SANCTUARY

TOILET (W)

TOILET (M)

WAITING ROOM 1

CLOSET

PULPIT

CHAPEL

STOREHOUSE

BENCH

AIR CONDITIONING OUTLET

FLOOR : BLACK GRANITE t 25
JET-BURNER FINISH

STAND
FOR FLOWERS

CHAIR

SLIT (INDIRECT LIGHTING)

H-SECTION STEEL
250×250×9×14
RUSTPROOF
FLUORINE RESIN COAT

STEEL STRUCTURED
COLUMN PL-38

0   3m
0   10ft

0   1m
0   3ft

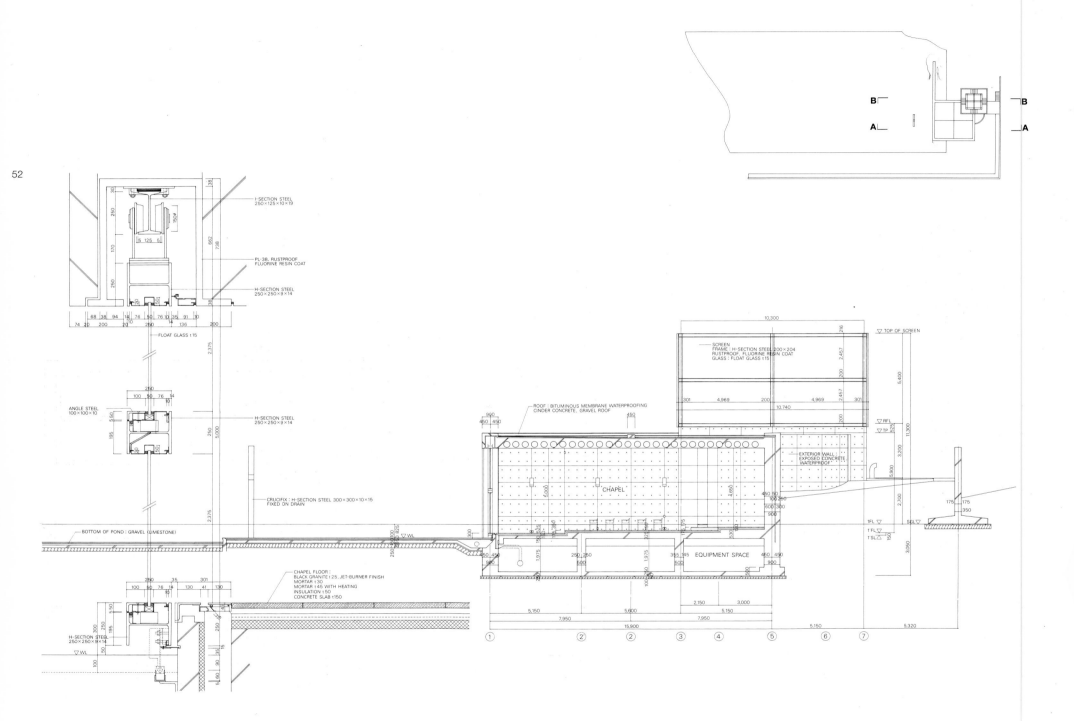

B — B

A — A

I-SECTION STEEL
250×125×10×19

PL-38, RUSTPROOF
FLUORINE RESIN COAT

H-SECTION STEEL
250×250×9×14

FLOAT GLASS t15

ANGLE STEEL
100×100×10

H-SECTION STEEL
250×250×9×14

CRUCIFIX : H-SECTION STEEL 300×300×10×15
FIXED ON DRAIN

BOTTOM OF POND : GRAVEL (LIMESTONE)

H-SECTION STEEL
250×250×9×14

▽ WL

CHAPEL FLOOR :
BLACK GRANITE t 25, JET-BURNER FINISH
MORTAR t 30
MORTAR t 45 WITH HEATING
INSULATION t 50
CONCRETE SLAB t150

SCREEN
FRAME : H-SECTION STEEL 200×204
RUSTPROOF, FLUORINE RESIN COAT
GLASS : FLOAT GLASS t15

ROOF : BITUMINOUS MEMBRANE WATERPROOFING
CINDER CONCRETE, GRAVEL ROOF

EXTERIOR WALL :
EXPOSED CONCRETE
WATERPROOF

CHAPEL

EQUIPMENT SPACE

▽ TOP OF SCREEN

▽ RFL

① ② ② ③ ④ ⑤ ⑥ ⑦

0   500mm

0   18in

0   5m

0   15ft

**Perspective of church and
details of movable screen**

53

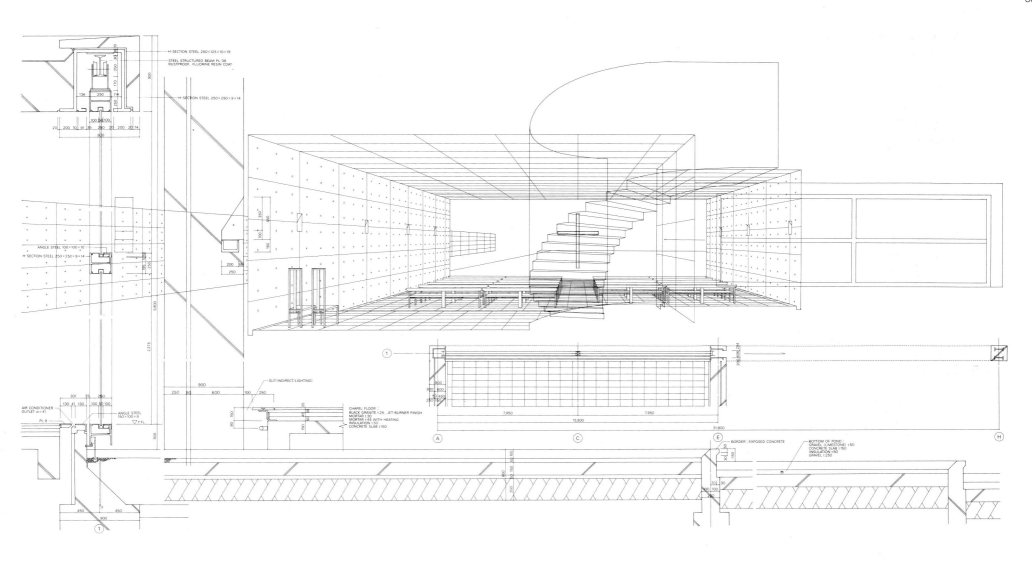

H-SECTION STEEL 250×125×10×19

STEEL STRUCTURED BEAM PL-38
RUSTPROOF, FLUORINE RESIN COAT

H-SECTION STEEL 250×250×9×14

ANGLE STEEL 100×100×10

H-SECTION STEEL 250×250×9×14

AIR CONDITIONER
OUTLET w=141

ANGLE STEEL
150×100×9

PL-9

SLIT (INDIRECT LIGHTING)

CHAPEL FLOOR :
BLACK GRANITE t 25, JET-BURNER FINISH
MORTAR t 30
MORTAR t 45 WITH HEATING
INSULATION t 50
CONCRETE SLAB t 150

BORDER : EXPOSED CONCRETE

BOTTOM OF POND :
GRAVEL (LIMESTONE) t 50
CONCRETE SLAB t 150
INSULATION t 50
GRAVEL t 250

0   500mm

0   18in

0   500mm

0   18in

54

0   1m

0   3ft

LAMINATED GLASS (FLOAT 8×12×12)

F.B. 9×50

BEAM : H-SECTION STEEL 425×250×6×9

CHANNEL STEEL 300×90×9×13

APPROACH CORRIDOR

250   250

500

H-SECTION STEEL 200×204×12×12
RUSTPROOF, FLUORINE RESIN COAT

FLOAT GLASS t15

SCREEN
FRAME : H-SECTION STEEL 200×204
RUSTPROOF, FLUORINE RESIN COAT
GLASS : FLOAT GLASS t15

SKYLIGHT : LAMINATED GLASS t 8+12+12
F.B. 9×50

FLOAT GLASS t6

BENCH

EXTERIOR WALL : EXPOSED CONCRETE,
WATERPROOF

WAITING
ROOM

LOBBY

WAITING
ROOM

PIT FOR POND WATER

MECHANICAL ROOM

TOP OF SCREEN

RFL
RSL

1FL
1SL

BFL
BSL

2,150   3,000   3,000   2,150

5,150   5,150

15,900

⑦   ⑥   ⑤   ④   ③   ①

1,950   1,200   4,500

0   3m

0   10ft

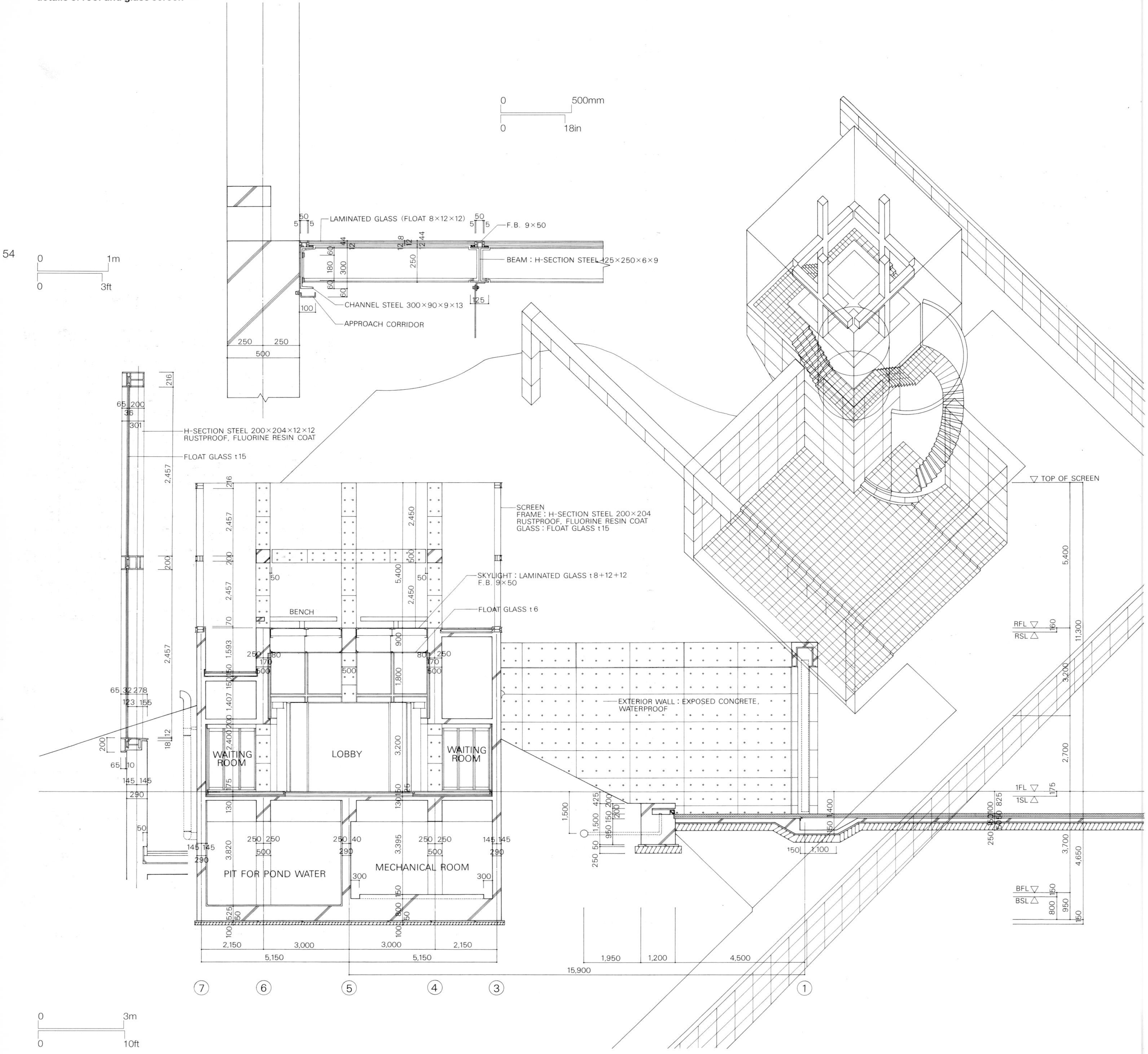

**Axonometric, roof plan and
details of glass screen**

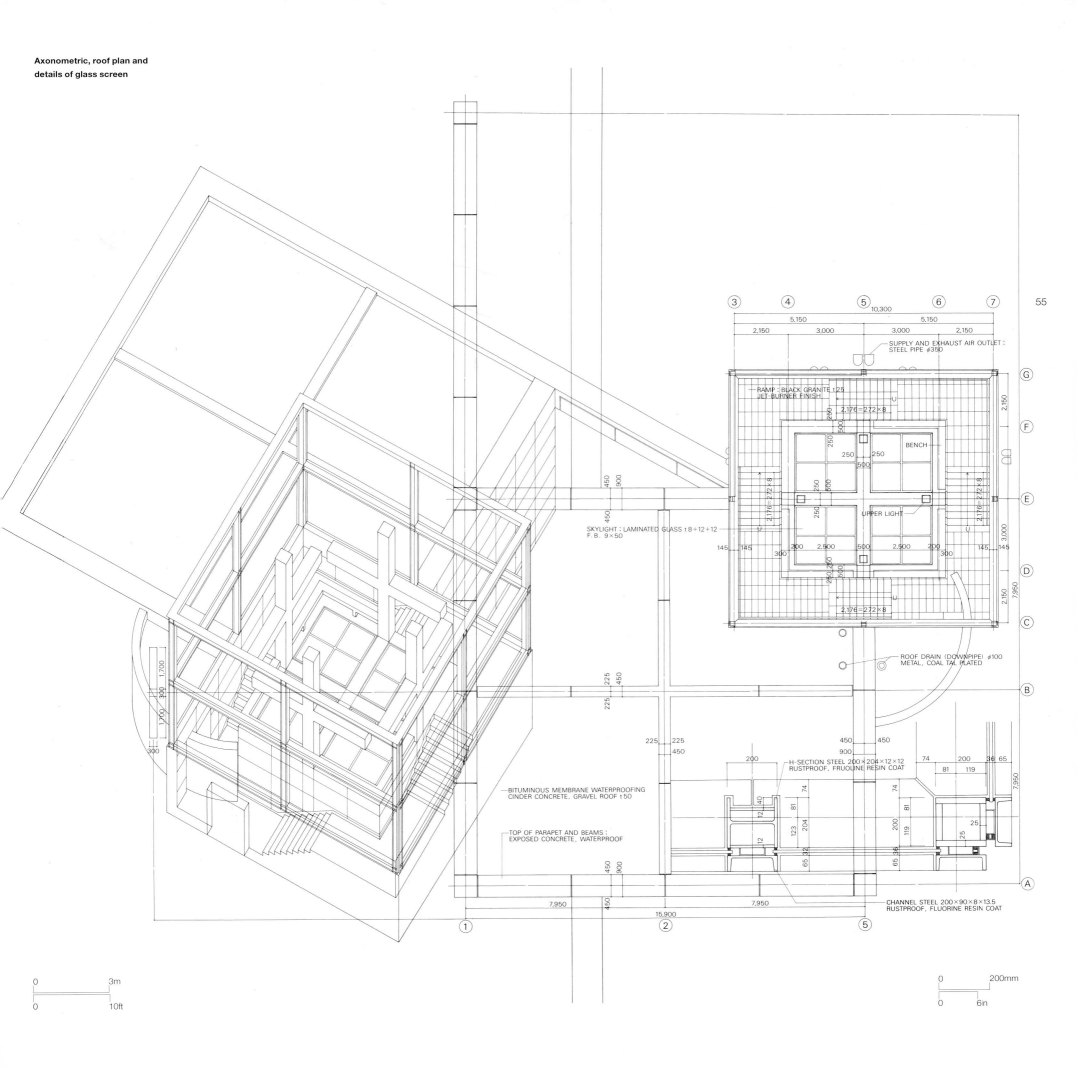

55

SUPPLY AND EXHAUST AIR OUTLET :
STEEL PIPE ⌀350

RAMP : BLACK GRANITE t 25
JET-BURNER FINISH

BENCH

UPPER LIGHT

SKYLIGHT : LAMINATED GLASS t 8+12+12
F. B. 9×50

2,176=272×8

ROOF DRAIN (DOWNPIPE) ⌀100
METAL, COAL TAL PLATED

H-SECTION STEEL 200×204×12×12
RUSTPROOF, FRUOLINE RESIN COAT

BITUMINOUS MEMBRANE WATERPROOFING
CINDER CONCRETE, GRAVEL ROOF t 50

TOP OF PARAPET AND BEAMS :
EXPOSED CONCRETE, WATERPROOF

CHANNEL STEEL 200×90×8×13.5
RUSTPROOF, FLUORINE RESIN COAT

0   3m
0   10ft

0   200mm
0   6in

Church of the Light

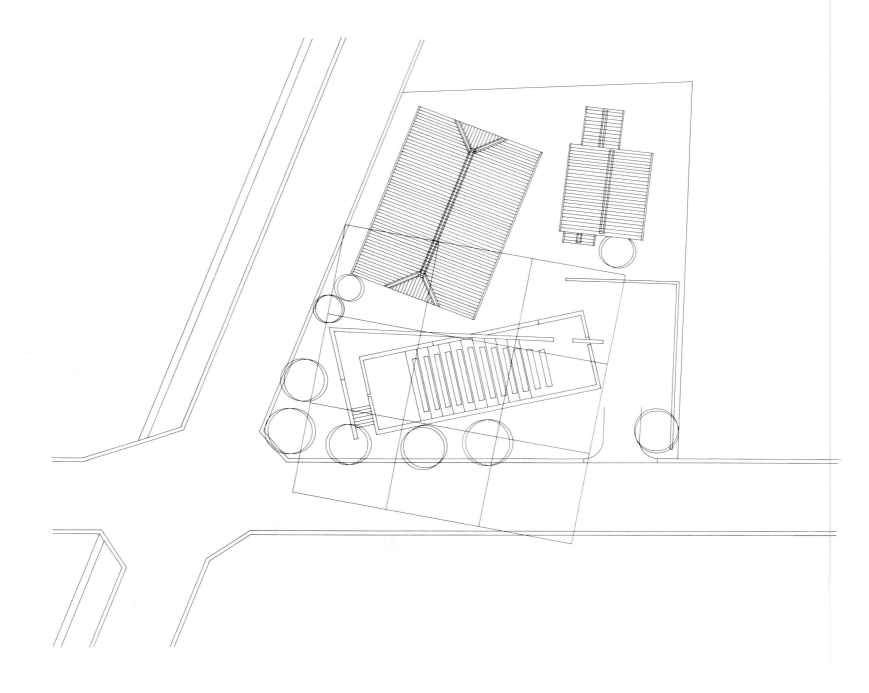

0   5m

0   15ft

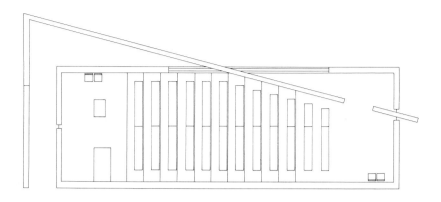

Floor plan

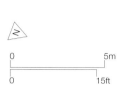

0   5m

0   15ft

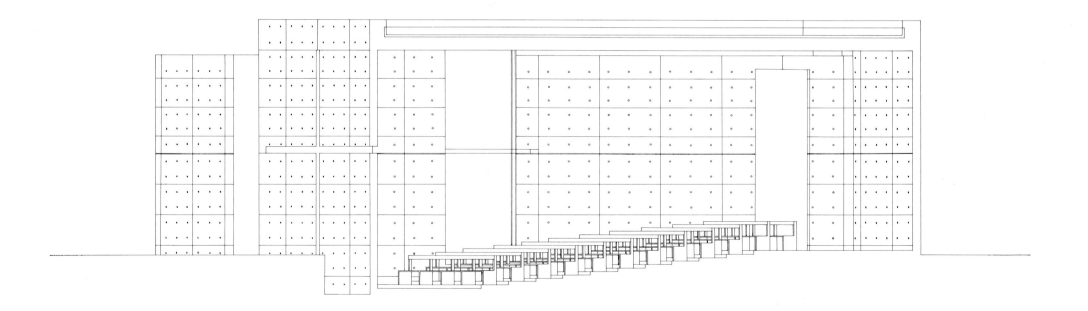

Section

0   2m

0   6ft

Perspective of church and details of entrance door

CEILING, WALL : EXPOSED CONCRETE
LIGHTING FITTINGS
FIXED FLOAT GLASS t6
FLOOR : BOARD t36 OIL STAIN FINISH (USED FOR TEMPORARY SCAFFOLD ON CONSTRUCTION SITE)
H=1,950
18,000
6,280
5,900
7,000
3,600
2,292
0
100mm
0
4in

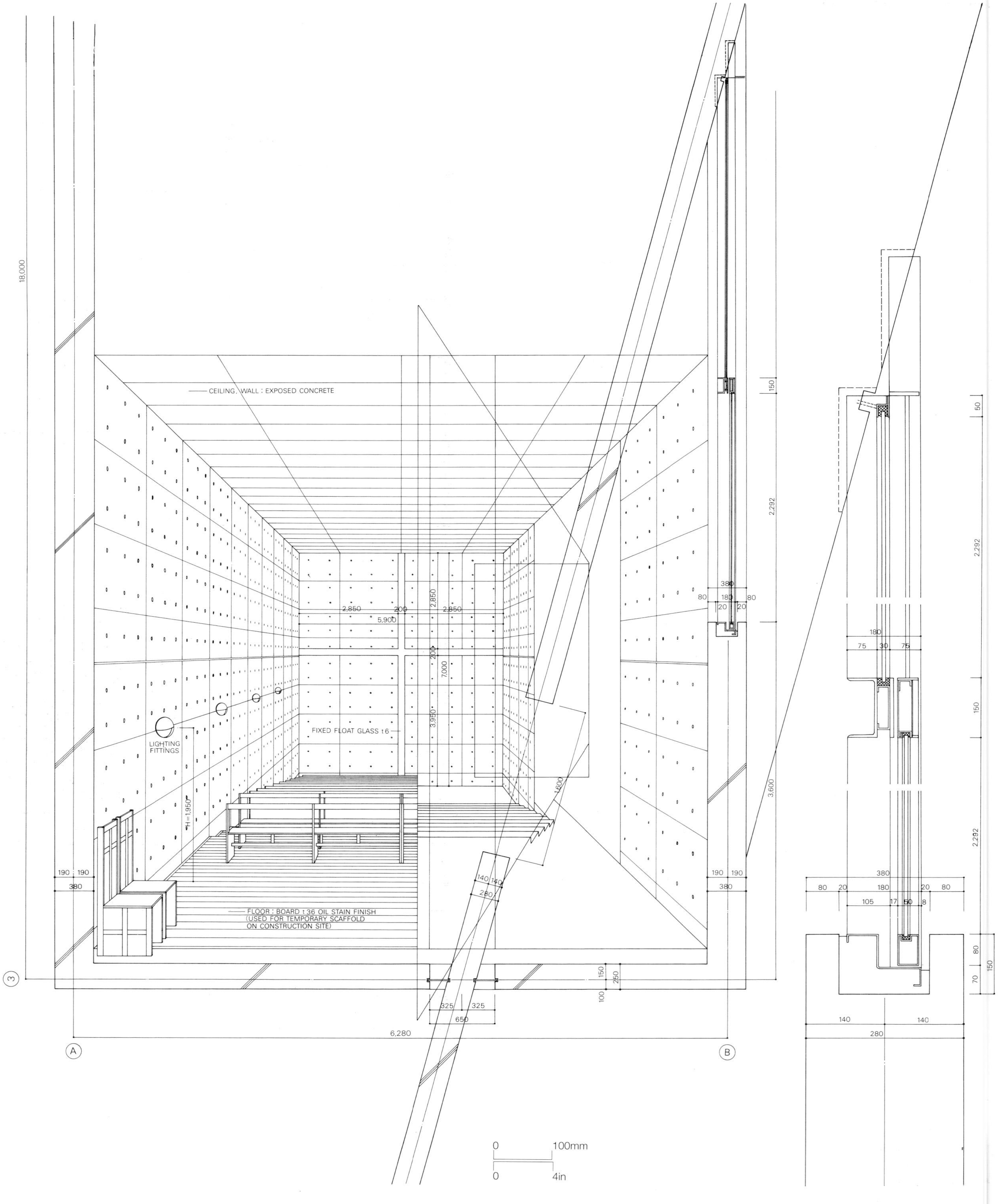

Perspective and details of furniture

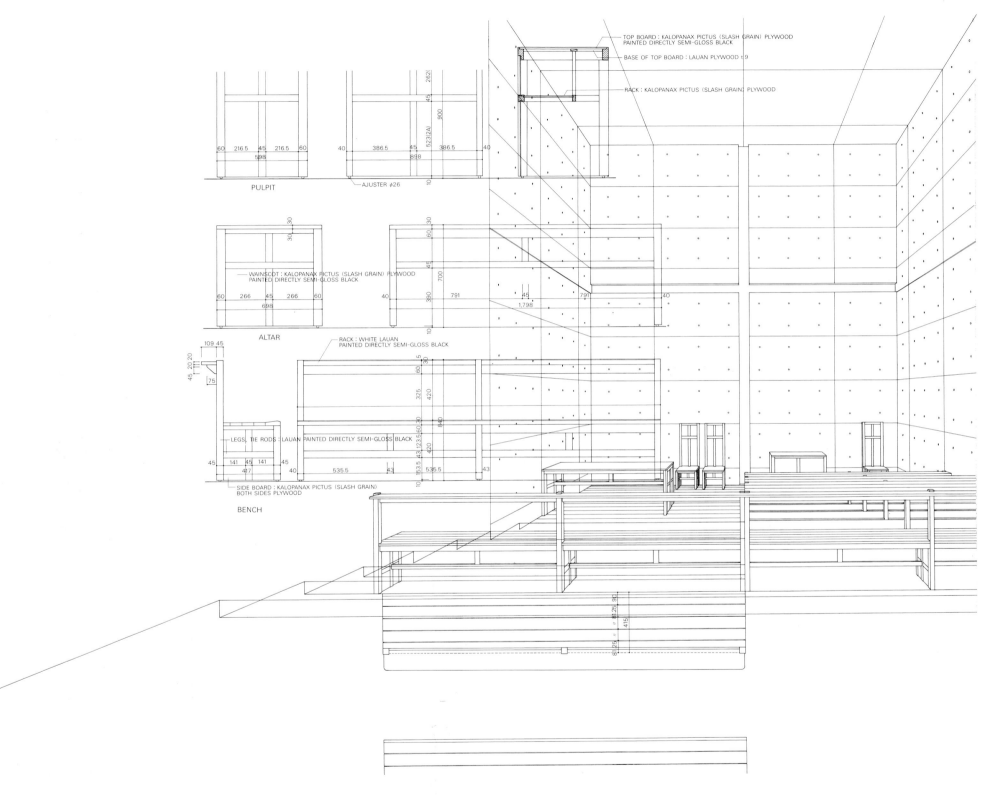

PULPIT

ALTAR

BENCH

TOP BOARD : KALOPANAX PICTUS (SLASH GRAIN) PLYWOOD PAINTED DIRECTLY SEMI-GLOSS BLACK

BASE OF TOP BOARD : LAUAN PLYWOOD t9

RACK : KALOPANAX PICTUS (SLASH GRAIN) PLYWOOD

AJUSTER ⌀26

WAINSCOT : KALOPANAX PICTUS (SLASH GRAIN) PLYWOOD PAINTED DIRECTLY SEMI-GLOSS BLACK

RACK : WHITE LAUAN PAINTED DIRECTLY SEMI-GLOSS BLACK

LEGS, TIE RODS : LAUAN PAINTED DIRECTLY SEMI-GLOSS BLACK

SIDE BOARD : KALOPANAX PICTUS (SLASH GRAIN) BOTH SIDES PLYWOOD

0 500mm
0 18in

Author's acknowledgements

60   I am indebted to Tadao Ando for his invaluable assistance, both in giving his time to explain each project, and in making it possible for me to visit the buildings. His office, in particular Hiromitsu Kuwata, helped with the drawings and supplied essential data, in addition to checking the draft of my essay.

Select bibliography

Books and periodicals: special issues

'Tadao Ando', *Japan Architect*, Tokyo, May 1982.
'Tadao Ando', *Japan Architect*, Tokyo, January 1991.
'Tadao Ando 1 1972–1987', *GA Architect*, No 8, Tokyo, 1987.
'Tadao Ando 2 1988–1993', *GA Architect*, No 12, Tokyo, 1993.
Tadao Ando Details, ADA Edita, Tokyo, 1991.
'Tadao Ando', *L'Architecture d'aujourd'hui*, No 255, February 1988.
Tadao Ando, Academy Editions Monograph No 14, London, 1990.
'Tadao Ando 1983–1990', *El Croquis*, No 44, Madrid, 1990.
'Tadao Ando 1989–1992', *El Croquis*, No 58, Madrid, 1993.
Tadao Ando: Beyond Horizons in Architecture, Tokyo, 1992.
Chaslin, François, *Tadao Ando – Minimalisme*, Paris, 1982.
Frampton, Kenneth (ed), *Tadao Ando: Buildings, Projects, Writings*, New York, 1984.
Frampton, Kenneth (ed), *Tadao Ando, The Yale Studio & Current Works*, New York, 1989.
Frampton, Kenneth (ed), *Tadao Ando*, The Museum of Modern Art, exhibition catalogue, New York, 1991.
Nitschke, Gunter, *From Shinto to Ando: Studies in Architectural Anthropology in Japan*, Academy Editions, London, 1993.

Tadao Ando: writings

'A wedge in circumstances', *Japan Architect*, 243, Vol 52, No 6, June 1977, pp 73–6.
'New relations between the space and the person', *Japan Architect*, No 247, October–November 1977, pp 43–6.
'Meet the architect: Tadao Ando', *GA Houses No 6*, Tokyo, October 1979, pp 172–205.
'From self-enclosed Modern architecture to Universality', *Japan Architect*, May 1982, p 6 ff.
'Representation and abstraction', *Japan Architect*, No 372, April 1988, p 8.
'Jun Port Island Building, 1985, and Kidosaki Residence, 1986', *Architectural Design*, Vol 58, No 5/6, 1988, pp 54–60.
'Abstraction serving reality', *Progressive Architecture*, Vol lxxi, No 2, February 1990, p 84.
'Collezione', *Japan Architect*, No 395, March 1990, pp 51–60.

Articles on the work of Tadao Ando

Akasaka, Yoshiaki, 'From confrontation to liberation: metamorphoses of spaces seen in the works of Tadao Ando', *Japan Architect*, No 342, October 1985, pp 27–9.
Bognar, Botond, 'Tadao Ando: a redefinition of Space, Time and Existence', *Architectural Design*, Vol 51, No 5, 1981, pp 25–6.
Bognar, Botond, 'Latest work of Tadao Ando', *Architectural Review*, Vol clxxii, No 1029, November 1982, pp 68–74.
'Chapel and Theatre on the Water', *Japan Architect*, No 272, April 1988, pp 43–51.
'Chapel on the Water' and 'Chapel of the Light', *Japan Architect*, No 386, June 1989, pp 6–17, 18–9.
'Church with the Light', *Japan Architect*, No 391–92, November–December 1989, pp 25–33.
Frampton, Kenneth, 'Synthesis of opposites', *L'Architecture d'aujourd'hui*, No 255, February 1988, pp 34–35.
Miyake, Kiichi, 'The path from Minimalism', *Japan Architect*, No 372, April 1988, pp 40–42.
Takeyama, Kiyoshi, 'Tadao Ando: heir to a tradition', *Perspecta*, No 20, Yale, 1983, pp 163–180.
'New version of the Old Row House', *Japan Architect*, No 243, Vol 52, No 6, June 1977, pp 57–64.
'Rose Garden', *Japan Architect*, 245, Vol 52, No 8, August 1977, pp 19–28.
Taki, Koji, 'The work of Fumihiko Maki and Tadao Ando', *Japan Architect*, No 319–320, November–December, 1983, pp 57–60.
Watanabe, Hiroshi, 'Tadao Ando: the architecture of denial,' *Japan Architect*, No 301, May 1982, pp 50–55.

Statistics

Church on the Water

Location: Tomamu, Yufutsu County, Hokkaido, Japan
Design: September 1985–April 1988
Construction: April 1988–September 1988
Structure: reinforced concrete, 1 storey, 1 basement
Site area: 6,730sq m
Building area: 344.9sq m
Total floor area: 520sq m
Structural engineer: Ascoral Engineering Associates
General contractor: Obayashi Corporation Co Ltd

Church of the Light

Location: Ibaraki, Osaka, Japan
Design: January 1987–May 1988
Construction: May 1988–April 1989
Structure: reinforced concrete, 1 storey
Site area: 836sq m
Building area: 113sq m
Total floor area: 113sq m
Structural engineer: Ascoral Engineering Associates
General contractor: Tatsumi Construction Co Ltd

Notes

1 Kenneth Frampton, *Modern Architecture: A Critical History*, London, 1980, p 297.
2 Kenneth Frampton, 'Towards a Critical Regionalism: six points for an architecture of resistance', in Hal Foster (ed), *The Anti Aesthetic: Essays on Postmodern Culture*, Washington DC, 1983, p 16.
3 *Modern Architecture: A Critical History*, op cit, p 297.
4 See Hiroshi Watanabe, 'Tadao Ando: the architecture of denial,' *Japan Architect*, No 301, May 1982, p 55.
5 Geometry provides the overall framework; this determines each aspect and the relationship to the landscape produced by its parts. Ando has stated: 'When, in this endeavour, the use of geometry centres on circles and squares – or their precise division, multiplication, diffusion, and transformation – the "architectural place" will respond, in reverberation, in this instance, regardless of this non-arbitrary character, condenses all varieties of meaning – or conversely, scatters it outward – transforming it endlessly.' from Tadao Ando, 'In dialogue with geometry: the creation of "landscape"', in 'Tadao Ando 1988–1993', *GA Architect*, No 12, Tokyo, 1993, p 25.
6 See Point 3: the free designing of the ground plan, Pierre Jeanneret: 'Five points towards a new architecture', 1926, in Ulrich Conrads, *Programmes and Manifestoes on 20th-Century Architecture*, London, 1970, pp 99–100.
7 *The Iliad of Homer*, translated by A Land, W Leaf and E Myers, Bk VII, pp 128, 211, 212.
8 J.B. Bury, *A History of Greece*, third edition, London, 1972, pp 472–4.
9 William Willets, *Chinese Art*, Vol 2, Harmondsworth, 1958, p 662.
10 From Kenneth Frampton, 'Synthesis of opposites', in *L'Architecture d'aujourd'hui*, February 1988, p 34.
11 Tadao Ando, 'Church on the Water', in *Japan Architect* Special issue, January 1991, p 110.
12 The Abbey at Sénanque, Provence, France, gave Ando an appreciation of the compelling power that springs from buildings when the architect contrives a unique logic for the architecture which is aligned with the logic latent in the surrounding land. Tadao Ando, 'In dialogue with geometry: the creation of "landscape"', *op cit*, p 24.